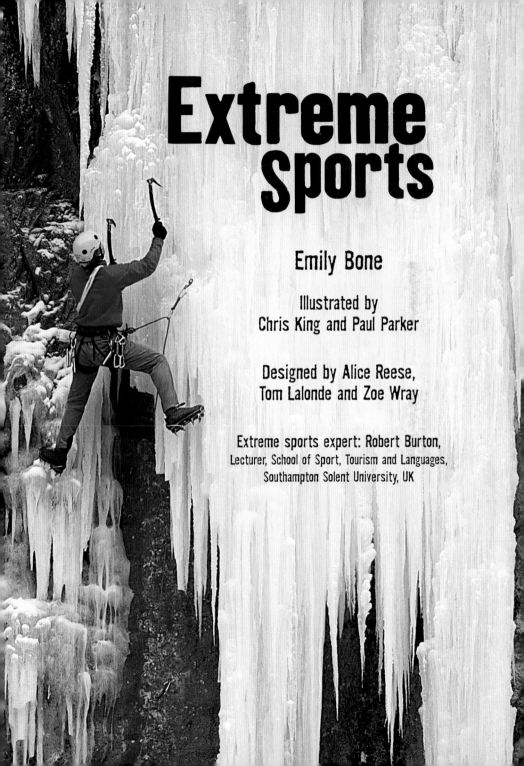

Extreme
Sports

Emily Bone

Illustrated by
Chris King and Paul Parker

Designed by Alice Reese,
Tom Lalonde and Zoe Wray

Extreme sports expert: Robert Burton,
Lecturer, School of Sport, Tourism and Languages,
Southampton Solent University, UK

Contents

This is a windsurfer doing a wave jump. Find out about extreme windsurfing on page 69.

What is an extreme sport?

Extreme sports are sports that involve a high level of danger – whether it's jumping from an aircraft, performing daring mid-air flips on a skateboard, or climbing up a sheer rock face.

Many extreme sports use specialized equipment, designed to keep people doing the sport safe. These free climbers rely on ropes and other safety equipment to stop them from falling. Find out how this works on pages 50-51.

Extreme wheels

Hurtling down a steep, muddy track, performing amazing mid-air tricks, or carefully balancing on obstacles, there are all kinds of extreme ways to ride a bike.

BMX

Short for 'bicycle motocross', BMX grew into a sport in the 1970s in California, USA, when children copied off-road motorcycle racing (motocross) by racing their bikes on dirt tracks.

These BMX cyclists are competing in a race. Find out more on pages 8-9.

This MTB competitor is taking part in a DH (downhill) event. Read more about MTB DH on pages 16-17.

MTB (mountain biking)

MTB (mountain biking) is the sport of riding specially modified bikes off road. This type of bike was first developed in 1896, when the U.S. army experimented with using them for military expeditions.

BMX racing

In a BMX race, riders speed through a track of bumps, jumps and berms (steep-sided bends) to reach the finish line first.

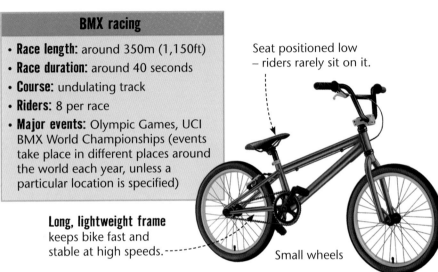

BMX racing

- **Race length:** around 350m (1,150ft)
- **Race duration:** around 40 seconds
- **Course:** undulating track
- **Riders:** 8 per race
- **Major events:** Olympic Games, UCI BMX World Championships (events take place in different places around the world each year, unless a particular location is specified)

Seat positioned low – riders rarely sit on it.

Long, lightweight frame keeps bike fast and stable at high speeds.

Small wheels

Course

This is a typical BMX track. The men's course is more challenging than the women's –15-20m (50-65ft) longer, with an extra ramped jump.

— Men's course

— Women's course

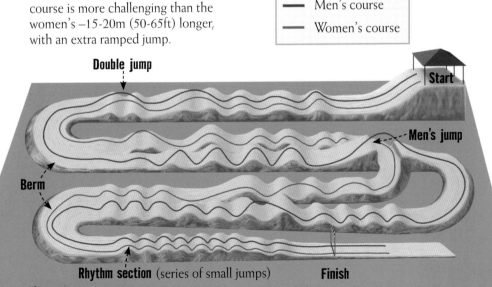

Double jump

Start

Men's jump

Berm

Rhythm section (series of small jumps)

Finish

Starting a race

Riders line up behind the starting gate. An announcer says: "OK riders, random start. Riders ready, watch the gate!"

Between three and five seconds later, the gate flies open, and riders push themselves down the start ramp.

Berm (steep-sided bend)

Here, riders can swoop (undertake) other riders on the inside of the bend. But doing a fast turn like this is tricky, and riders often crash.

Rhythm section

This is a series of low jumps or bumps. Riders **roll-through**, **manual**, or **jump** them.

Manual – lifting up the front wheel

Jump – both wheels in the air

Roll-through – both wheels on the ground

Finish

It's unusual for all riders to reach the finish line.

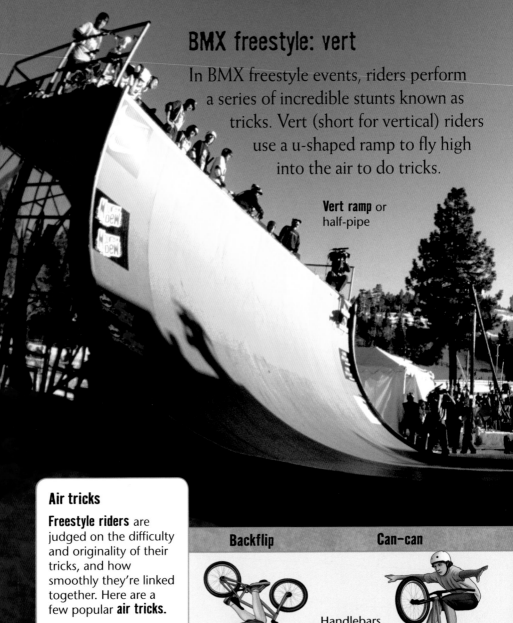

BMX freestyle: vert

In BMX freestyle events, riders perform a series of incredible stunts known as tricks. Vert (short for vertical) riders use a u-shaped ramp to fly high into the air to do tricks.

Vert ramp or half-pipe

Air tricks

Freestyle riders are judged on the difficulty and originality of their tricks, and how smoothly they're linked together. Here are a few popular **air tricks.**

Backflip

Bike and rider flip backwards in a complete circle.

Can-can

Handlebars are held between legs and body, and arms are stretched out.

This is a BMX vert competitor doing a **180° air trick**, where the rider and bike spin 180° (a semi-circle) before landing back on the ramp.

The top edge of the ramp is called the **coping**. Riders start their tricks from here.

Riders can jump up to 4.5m (15ft) above the ramp.

No hander

One leg is flipped over the bike frame...

...then stretched out to the side.

Superman

Legs are held away from the pedals.

BMX vert

- **Venue:** vert ramp, often in a skatepark
- **Competition:** individual runs lasting 30 seconds, assessed by a team of judges
- **Major events:** BMX Big Air, X Games, BMX Worlds, World Extreme Games

BMX freestyle: others

Along with vert, there are four other types of BMX freestyle – dirt, street, park and flatland.

BMX Dirt

- **Venue:** dirt mounds
- **Competition:** 3 jumps
- **Major events:** Red Bull Empire of Dirt

Dirt riders perform air tricks while jumping between dirt mounds.

This is the **nothing trick**, where the rider lets go of the bike while he's in the air.

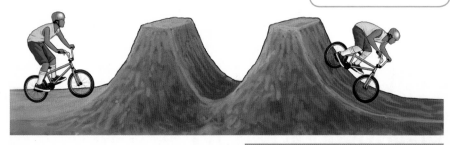

BMX Street

- **Venue:** any street, or street obstacles in a skate park
- **Competition:** runs lasting up to 45 seconds
- **Major events:** X Games, X Fest, Dew Tour

Street riders make up a run (routine) where they hop, jump and slide down obstacles such as walls, railings and steps.

BMX freestyle bikes have **pegs**, which are used in tricks called grinds.

This is a **handrail grind**, where the rider slides down a railing on pegs.

This berm is part of a XC race in British Columbia, Canada. MTB bikes are lightweight, strong and efficient, to cope with climbs and obstacles like this one.

Some XC courses are built for a particular race. This is the XC course made specially for the 2012 Olympic Games in the UK. It's only 4.8km (2.9 miles) long, so competitors do 10 laps.

XC MTB

- **Race length:** 40-50km (25-30 miles)
- **Race duration:** around 2 hours
- **Course:** rough forest paths and mountain trails
- **Riders:** any number
- **Major events:** Olympic Games, UCI World Championships

Gap or ramp?: Mo… riders **jump** acros… the rocky **gap** as … is the faster rout… crash landing cou… seriously damage… bike, meaning th… the race is over.

Signs

Signs along the route tell riders which way to go and warn them what's coming up ahead.

↑	Straight on	→	Right turn
←	Left turn	✕	Wrong way
‖	Bridge	≋	Water crossing
↓↓	Downhill		
↓↓↓	Steep or rocky downhill		

Rocky roads: **Triple Trouble, Deane's Drop** and **The Rock Garden** are steep, boulder-strewn sections.

They include short paths with dangerous rocky drops...

...or smoother, longer paths that could cost valuable seconds.

areas

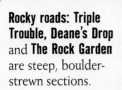

Perhaps the safer, but slower, **ramp** is the better option.

Ramp

y gap

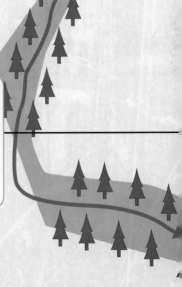

Uphill: Strenuous uphill stretches such as **Snake Hill** and **The Breathtaker** are littered with rocks. Riders stay seated to conserve energy.

Flatlanders make the bike spin and balance in a variety of positions without setting foot on the ground. Here are some popular tricks:

BMX Flatland

- **Venue:** anywhere with a flat, hard surface
- **Competition:** several runs lasting for a specified length of time – e.g. 2 minutes
- **Major events:** Flatland World Circuit, Red Bull Flatland Voodoo Jam (USA)

Boomerang
Swinging around in front of the handlbars, then back to the seat.

Endo
Balancing on the front or back wheel.

Barhop
Hopping over the handlebars to land on the front pegs.

Riders in park events perform runs of air, street and flatland tricks on obstacles in a skate or BMX park.

BMX Park

- **Venue:** skatepark or purpose-built BMX park
- **Competition:** runs lasting up to 40 seconds
- **Major events:** X Games, X Fest, Dew Tour

Spine
2 quarter-pipes back-to-back

Quarter-pipe
A ramp (quarter of a half-pipe)

Half-pipe

Pyramid
Ramps leading up to a flat 'table'

MTB XC (cross-country)

MTB (mountain bike) races are longer than BMX ones, and done over rougher terrain. XC (cross-country) MTB races are some of the longest and toughest, as there are lots of difficult obstacles for cyclists to overcome.

Finish: The first rider over the finish line after 10 laps is the winner.

Pit: If a rider has a problem with his bike he pulls into the pits to get it fixed. This is also the place to pick up energy drinks and gels.

The Breathtaker

Here, a tunnel
er itself. It's a
see how far
hey are.

Downhill: Riders have to be extra careful on downhill drops such as the **Leap of Faith**. If they go too fast, they'll lose control and skid off-course.

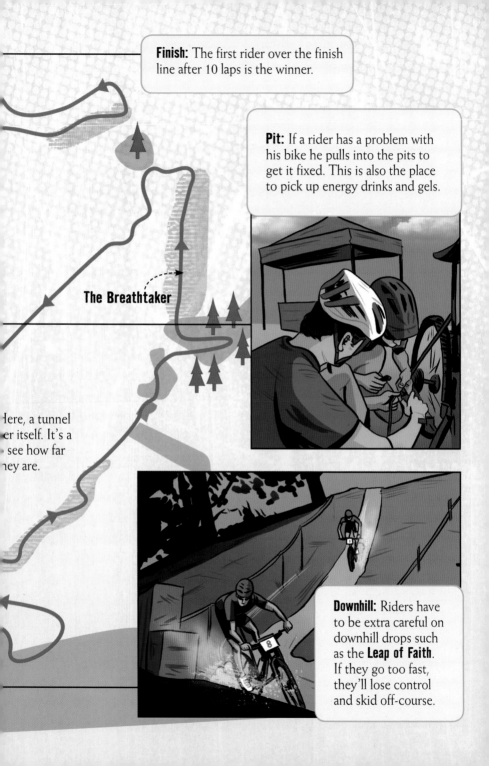

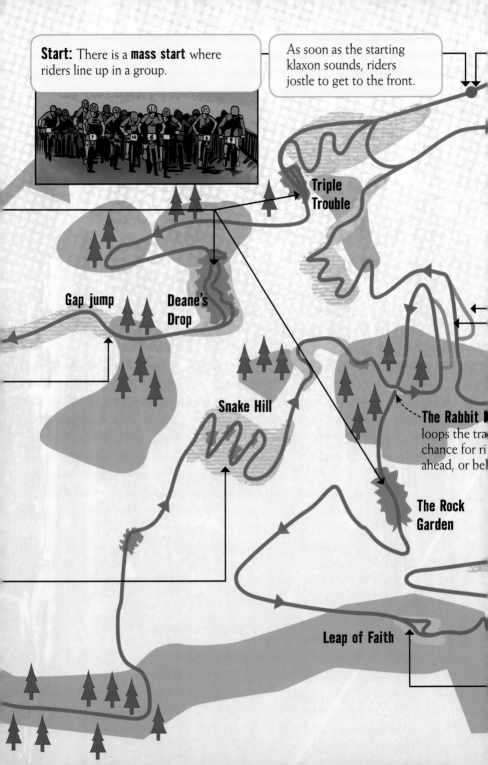

Start: There is a **mass start** where riders line up in a group.

As soon as the starting klaxon sounds, riders jostle to get to the front.

Triple Trouble

Gap jump

Deane's Drop

Snake Hill

The Rabbit H
loops the tra
chance for ri
ahead, or be

The Rock Garden

Leap of Faith

MTB DH (downhill)

In a DH event, riders hurl themselves, one-by-one, down a steep course, over a series of jumps, bumps and berms. It's a nerve-wracking race against the clock – the fastest from top to bottom wins.

MTB DH

- **Race length:** 1.5-3.5km (0.9-2.2 miles)
- **Race duration:** 2-5 minutes
- **Course:** downhill track
- **Riders:** any number
- **Major events:** UCI Mountain Bike World Cup (Fort William, Scotland, UK), Crankworx (Whistler, Canada), Megavalanche (The Alps, France), Sea Otter Classic (California, USA)

1. Start

Competitors ride up to the starting hut when their name is called.

Suspension at front and rear helps to absorb shocks as the bike bumps down the course.

Full-face helmet and goggles

Body padding

Full-finger gloves

Protective pads

This bike has **fat, thick-tread wheels** to help it grip the muddy course. Narrower, smoother treads are for dry courses.

A klaxon sounds and the race starts. The competitor pedals hard and speeds downhill.

2. Jump

Riders jump over obstacles such as tree roots, ramps and boulders. Both the rider and bike fly into the air.

The rider hunches down to keep the jump low.

3. Berm

During a berm, the rider pedals hard and leans into the bend.

This path is called a line.

4. Turns

Cutting across turns saves valuable seconds.

5. Finish

There's a big jump into the finish line. An electronic timer records each rider's time.

MTB trials

MTB trials competitors navigate a course littered with tricky obstacles. Superior bike handling and balance skills are essential.

This trials rider has just completed a move called a **rear wheel hop** to get from a lower to a higher obstacle.

Unlike other MTBs, trials bikes don't have seats. The rider doesn't need one, and it could get in the way.

Obstacles can be anything – concrete blocks, walls and tubes, rocks, tree trunks or even vehicle parts.

MTB trials

- **Course:** 1.5-2km (0.9-1.25 miles) with a minimum of 12 difficult sections (a difficult section is a series of obstacles)
- **Competitors:** any number
- **Major events:** UCI Trials World Championships

Trial moves

Trials riders must learn these moves to help them hop up, move along and hop off different obstacles.

Trackstand

Rider and bike balance so they're completely still.

Endo turn

Turning on the front wheel allows the rider to turn on narrow ledges.

Side hop

The rider hops on his wheels to build up power, before jumping up sideways onto an obstacle.

Pedal kick

To jump over a gap, the rider hops on his back wheel...

Then, he kicks (pushes) forwards.

Points

Penalty points are given each time a rider puts a foot on the ground. This is known as '**dabbing**'.

- **1 point** is given for one foot.
- **5 points** for both feet.
- The rider with the **fewest points** at the end wins.

Air extremes

Leaping from a plane or high platform with just a
canopy (parachute) or glider to break your fall,
extreme sports done in the air are some
of the most exhilarating, and risky.

Skydiving

Skydivers jump out of
aircraft with skydiving
equipment strapped to their backs.
They fall at speeds of up to 190km/h
(120mph), before releasing canopies to slow
themselves down and glide to the ground.

Skydiving

- **Records: first jump:** Leslie Irwin (USA), April 19, 1919, California, USA
- **Highest jump:** Felix Baumgartner (Austria), 38,969.3m (127,852ft), October 14, 2012, over New Mexico, USA
- **Largest freefall formation:** 400 people, February 8, 2006, over Udon Thani, Thailand
- **Major events:** World Air Games, FAI World Parachuting Championships

These skydivers are doing a formation jump. They jump out of a plane as a group and form shapes with their bodies as they fall.

Up, up, and away!

Preparation before a skydive is just as important as the jump itself.

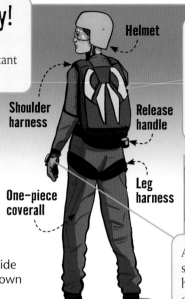

Helmet

Shoulder harness

Release handle

One-piece coverall

Leg harness

Inside: main canopy (parachute), deployment bag, reserve canopy (in case main canopy fails), pilot chute and lines.

1. Equipment

Skydivers carefully check all their equipment, then pack it inside a backpack called a **container**.

The equipment inside the container is known as a **rig**.

An **altimeter** tells skydivers their height from the ground at all times.

2. In the air

A plane lifts a group of divers to around 4,000m (13,000ft). When the plane is flying over the **dropzone (DZ)**, a green light flashes in the cabin.

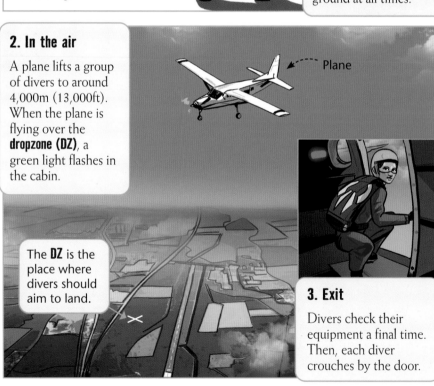

Plane

The **DZ** is the place where divers should aim to land.

3. Exit

Divers check their equipment a final time. Then, each diver crouches by the door.

The diver counts herself out by calling "Up, down, arch!" Then, she falls.

This part of the dive is called the **freefall**.

4. Deployment

At around 760m (2,500ft), they pull the **release handle**. This deploys, or releases, the **pilot chute**, which drags the **deployment bag** and **lines** from the container.

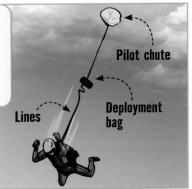

Pilot chute

Lines

Deployment bag

The **pilot chute** pulls the **main canopy** from the **deployment bag**. Wind inflates the canopy.

Pilot chute

A device called a **slider** stops the **main canopy** from opening too quickly.

Toggles

5. Landing

Before landing, the diver pulls on the **toggles**. These are like brakes – they slow the fall by changing the shape of the canopy. Then, the diver glides gently to the ground.

The highest jump

On October 14, 2012, extreme athlete, Felix Baumgartner, attempted the highest ever skydive. He jumped from an incredible 39km (24 miles) above New Mexico, USA, with just a canopy to break his fall.

This is a picture of Felix as he started his jump.

This capsule lifted Felix into the sky. It supplied oxygen and also protected him against the cold. Cameras to film the jump were attached to the capsule.

Helmet with earphones and microphone to communicate with the ground control team

Spacesuit to protect Felix's body and supply oxygen during the jump

Cameras on each leg

How it happened

1. A huge, helium-filled balloon lifted the capsule with Felix inside. It took 3 hours to reach the correct height.

2. His ground control team radioed the command, "Ready to jump!"

3. Felix opened the capsule door, stepped to the edge...

...and jumped.

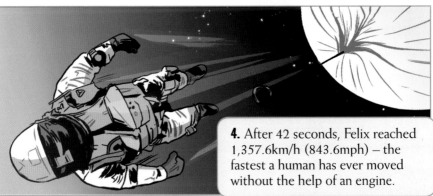

4. After 42 seconds, Felix reached 1,357.6km/h (843.6mph) – the fastest a human has ever moved without the help of an engine.

5. A minute later, disaster struck, as Felix started to spin rapidly. But, 23 seconds later, he managed to regain control.

6. At 1,500m (4,920ft), after 4 minutes 19 seconds of freefall, Felix deployed his canopy. Soon after, he landed safely.

BASE jumping

A more extreme, higher-risk version of skydiving, BASE jumps are low parachute jumps. BASE stands for the different objects or platforms that are jumped from: building, antenna, span (bridge) and earth (cliff, quarry, gorge or mountain).

These BASE jumpers are starting their jumps from a mountain (earth platform) in Norway.

BASE jumping

- **Records: Highest jump:** 7,220m (23,690ft), Mount Everest's north face, Nepal, Valery Rozov (Russia), May 5, 2013
- **Lowest jump:** 31.1m (102ft), St. Paul's Cathedral, UK, Russell Powell (UK), 1990
- **Major events:** ProBASE, KL tower BASE (Malaysia), Bridge Day (New River Gorge Bridge, West Virginia, USA)

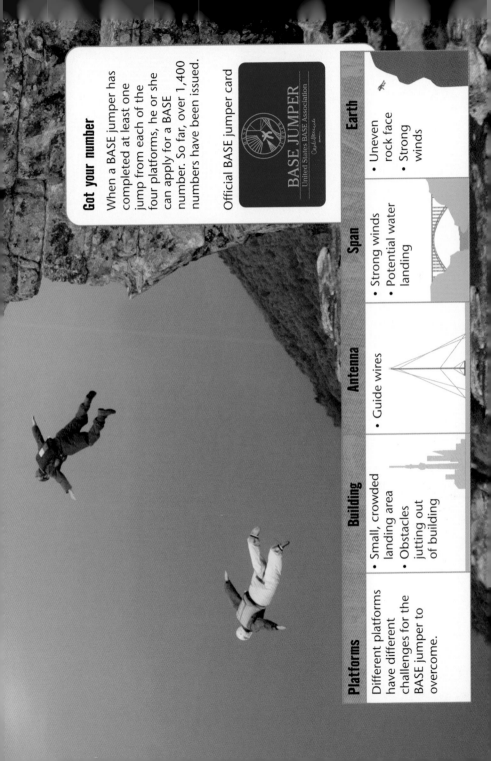

Got your number

When a BASE jumper has completed at least one jump from each of the four platforms, he or she can apply for a BASE number. So far, over 1,400 numbers have been issued.

Official BASE jumper card

BASE JUMPER
United States BASE Association

Platforms	Building	Antenna	Span	Earth
Different platforms have different challenges for the BASE jumper to overcome.	• Small, crowded landing area • Obstacles jutting out of building	• Guide wires	• Strong winds • Potential water landing	• Uneven rock face • Strong winds

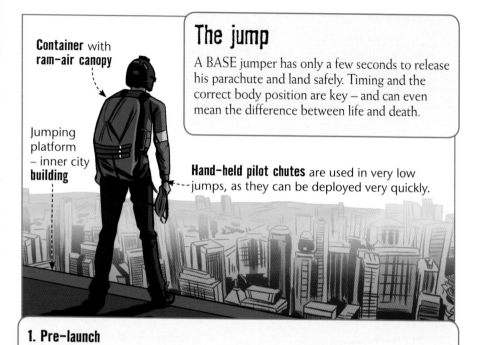

Container with **ram-air canopy**

Jumping platform – inner city building

The jump

A BASE jumper has only a few seconds to release his parachute and land safely. Timing and the correct body position are key – and can even mean the difference between life and death.

Hand-held pilot chutes are used in very low jumps, as they can be deployed very quickly.

1. Pre-launch

Only experienced skydivers BASE jump. Jumpers should complete more than 200 skydives, then undergo extensive BASE jump training.

2. Launch

The jumper launches himself away from the jumping platform, facing the ground.

3. Freefall

During **freefall**, he brings his arms down, and arches his back. His body 'cups' the air, forcing him forward, so he's a safe distance from the building.

This is called **tracking**.

He deploys the **pilot chute**...

4. Deploy

At 300m (1,000ft), it's time to release the canopy.

BASE jumpers use a modified ram-air canopy design that opens more quickly as air shoots, or 'rams', into the cells.

...which drags open the **main canopy**.

Control lines

The main canopy opens and slows the jumper's fall. He steers left or right by pulling on **control lines**.

5. Landing

There's not much space in a city, so it's important to steer and land in exactly the right place.

Wingsuit flying

Wearing a modified jumpsuit with added 'wings', a wingsuit flyer freefalls for as long as possible during a skydive or BASE jump. A canopy opens before landing.

How does it work?

A wingsuit makes the diver's body into a shape similar to a plane or bird's wing – curved on top and flatter underneath.

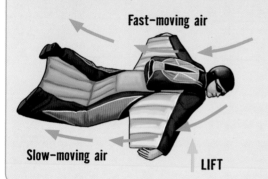

Fast-moving air

Slow-moving air

LIFT

Air flows over and under the wingsuit. It moves **faster** over it, and **slower** underneath it.

The slower moving air creates a force called **lift**. This pushes up the diver so he falls less quickly than a normal skydiver.

Flying

By changing the shape of his or her body, a wingsuit flyer can steer or 'fly' through the air.

To fly forward...

The diver lifts his legs, to increase the curved shape of his body.

To fly sideways...

The right arm and leg are lifted up to go left. The left arm and leg are lifted to move right.

To dive...

Arms move closer to the body and the legs come together. This decreases lift.

The air moves even slower here, increasing lift.

A group of wingsuit flyers is called a flock.

Camera

Wingsuit flying

- **Records: Highest ever jump:** 11,358m (37,265ft), Jhonathan Florez (Columbia), Columbia, April 21, 2012
  Greatest horizontal distance during a jump: 26.9km (16.7 miles), Shin Ito (Japan), California, USA, May 26, 2012
- **Major events:** Wingsuit World Championships, Artistic Wingsuit Competition

Wings are made from extra material sewn between each arm and body, and between the legs.

Bungee crane

Bungee cage

Cord

Bungee jumping

- **Records: Highest ever jump (from a hot-air balloon):** 4,632m (15,200ft), Curtis Rivers (UK), Puertollano, Spain
- **Highest fixed jump in use:** 233m (764ft, 5in), Macau Tower, China

Bungee

Bungee jumpers leap from a high platform while attached to a thick, rubber cord. The cord stretches as the jumper falls, then it snaps back, shooting the jumper back up into the air.

Essential equipment

Bungee jumpers must have the right equipment fitted before jumping.

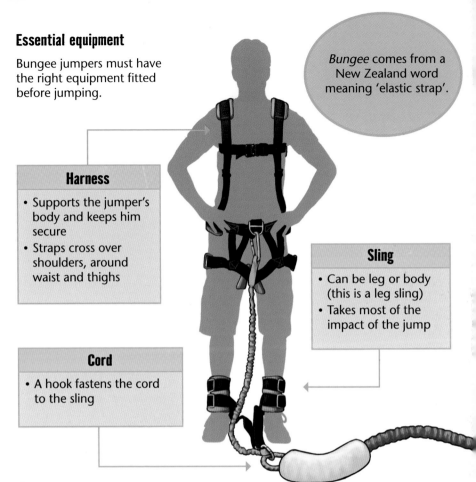

Bungee comes from a New Zealand word meaning 'elastic strap'.

Harness

- Supports the jumper's body and keeps him secure
- Straps cross over shoulders, around waist and thighs

Sling

- Can be leg or body (this is a leg sling)
- Takes most of the impact of the jump

Cord

- A hook fastens the cord to the sling

Jumps

Different harnesses and cords are used for different types of jump:

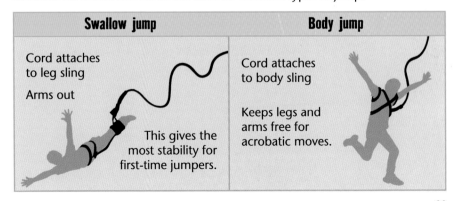

Swallow jump

Cord attaches to leg sling

Arms out

This gives the most stability for first-time jumpers.

Body jump

Cord attaches to body sling

Keeps legs and arms free for acrobatic moves.

Gliders

Using a canopy or 'wing' to glide for hours in the sky, hang glides and paraglides are like longer, slower skydives. Hang gliders fly a v-shaped wing. Paragliders use a wing canopy similar to a large parachute.

Wing
Made from lightweight tubes with nylon fabric stretched over them.

The hang gliding wing design was first developed by NASA as a way to fly spacecraft back to Earth.

Pod harness
Full-body harness that encloses the upper body and legs, leaving the arms free.

Pilot

Control bar
The pilot uses this to steer the wing by shifting his or her body weight left or right. Pulling the bar backward or forward changes the speed.

Hang gliding

- **Records: Greatest distance**: 704km (437 miles), Michael Barber (USA), Texas, USA, June 19, 2002
- **Highest flight:** 11,826m (38,000ft), Judy Leden (UK), Jordan, October 25, 1994
- **Major events:** XC League, World Hang Gliding Championships

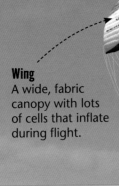

Wing
A wide, fabric canopy with lots of cells that inflate during flight.

Paragliding

- **Records: Greatest distance:** 502.9km (312.5 miles), Nevil Hulett (South Africa), South Africa, December 14, 2008
- **Highest flight:** 4,526m (14,849ft), Robbie Whittall (UK), South Africa, January 6, 1993
- **Major events:** Paragliding World Cup, X-Alps, Acro World Cup, Accuracy World Cup

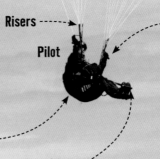

Risers

Pilot

Brakes
Lines attached to the edges of the wing. The pilot pulls on these to steer, adjust speed, and go up and down.

Harness
The pilot is strapped into a seat and stays in a seated position.

Speed bar
By pushing on this bar with his or her feet, the pilot changes the angle of the wing and increases speed.

Different moves

Here you can see how hang gliders and paragliders launch, fly and land.

Hang gliding

1. Launch
The pilot runs down a gentle slope. Air rushes around the wing and lifts it up.

As the wing lifts up, the pilot tucks her legs inside the harness.

2. Steering
With her hands on the control bar, the pilot shifts her weight left or right to steer in those directions.

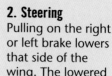

Paragliding

1. Launch
Facing the wing, the pilot pulls on the risers. This forces wind into the wing, so it inflates and rises up.

This is called **kiting.**

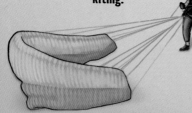

2. Steering
Pulling on the right or left brake lowers that side of the wing. The lowered side flies slower, so the wing turns.

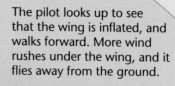

The pilot looks up to see that the wing is inflated, and walks forward. More wind rushes under the wing, and it flies away from the ground.

3. Flying

Rising columns of air, called **thermals** and **lifts**, keep paragliders and hang gliders flying.

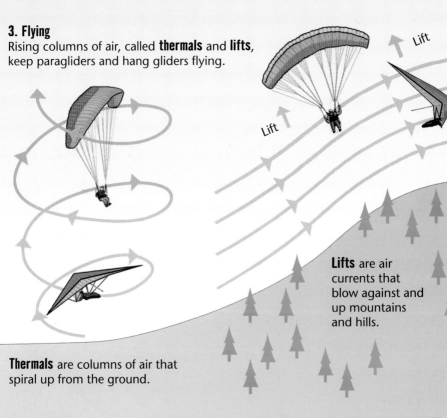

Lift

Lift

Lift

Lifts are air currents that blow against and up mountains and hills.

Thermals are columns of air that spiral up from the ground.

4. Landing

Pushing the control bar forward raises the front of the wing and stops air from flowing over it. This decreases lift and the wing drops down.

Pulling down both brakes lowers the sides of the wing. This deflates it so it gently floats to the ground.

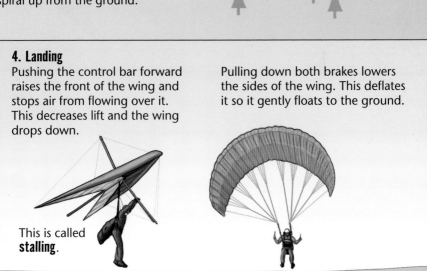

This is called **stalling**.

Let's go fly a kite

Kite buggying uses wind power to pull a buggy, very fast, along the ground. A kite buggy can easily reach speeds in excess of 130km/h (80mph).

The **kite** is a wide canopy. The driver uses **control lines** to steer the kite and catch as much wind as possible.

Kite buggying

- **Records: Fastest speed:** 135.34km/h (84.10mph), Brian Holgate (USA), California, USA, March 6, 2012
- **Greatest distance:** 1035km (643.11 miles), Stefan Berkner (Germany), Denmark, August 1, 2013

Control lines are held by the pilot or attached to a body harness. Pulling on these changes the shape and position of the kite.

Kite buggies need a wide, flat area with strong winds. Long beaches, like this one in Oregon, USA, are popular kite buggying areas.

- - - The **pilot** is strapped into the buggy.

Foot pegs are for steering. They're also used to brake and slide.

Tricks

Buggyers do amazing jumps, spins and slides, called tricks.

Twister

Using the control lines, the pilot makes wind rush into the kite. The buggy jumps off the ground and spins 360°.

Wheelstand

The pilot leans in the direction of the kite and steers it to catch a little wind. This tilts the buggy up onto 2 wheels.

Slide

The buggy is steered in the opposite direction of the kite, so it skids sideways along the ground.

Spin

Similar to a slide, but the buggy is steered in a complete circle.

39

This is a **grind trick** (go to pages 44-45 to find out more about tricks).

On your skates

For over 60 years, people have been riding and performing tricks on skateboards. Today, skateboarding is one of the most popular extreme sports, with millions of skaters worldwide.

Street skateboarders do tricks on obstacles in city streets or skate parks.

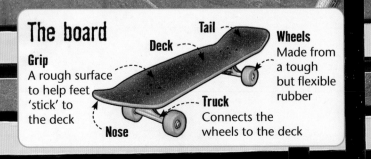

The board

Grip
A rough surface to help feet 'stick' to the deck

Nose

Deck

Tail

Truck
Connects the wheels to the deck

Wheels
Made from a tough but flexible rubber

Similar to BMX vert, **vert skateboarders** use a vertical ramp or half-pipe as a way to gain height for air tricks.

When a skateboard has all four wheels off the ground, it's called **catching air**.

Skateboarding

- **Records: highest and longest jump (from a vert ramp):** height: 7.16m (23.5ft), distance: 24m (79ft), Danny Way (USA), California, USA, June 19, 2004
- **Fastest speed:** 130.08km/h (80.83mph), Mischo Erban (Canada), Colorado, USA, September 31, 2010
- **Major events:** X Games, AST Dew Tour, Vans Warped Tour

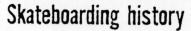

Skateboarding history

Ever since it began, the sport of skateboarding has been shaped by people who have invented new equipment, obstacles and tricks.

1. Sidewalk surfing (1950s–60s)

The first skateboards were made by surfers, so they could 'surf' the streets when there were no waves.

Skateboards had thin, flat decks and clay wheels.

2. New materials (1970s)

In 1972, skater Frank Nasworthy invented a synthetic skate wheel. This gave better grip, so skaters could experiment with more complex tricks.

With their new wheels, skaters began to ride the walls of empty swimming pools – the first 'vert' ramps.

This trick, called the **ollie**, was invented in 1976 (see page 44 for how it's done).

Other skaters took to the streets, making up tricks on whatever obstacles they could find.

3. Skate stars (1980–90s)

During the 80s and 90s, many of the best skaters became famous for inventing, then perfecting, difficult new tricks that were copied by other skaters.

Street skater Rodney Mullen invented around 30 **flip tricks**, where the skater jumps and spins the board.

Mark Gonzales was the first to **grind** handrails, now a popular street trick.

Vert pro Tony Hawk invented over 80 **air tricks.**

4. The modern skater (2000–present)

Now, there are thousands of skateparks across the world, where skaters can practice tricks. They can also get tips and share skating videos with other skaters online.

Skate tricks

There are thousands of skateboarding tricks to learn, but most fall into these categories:

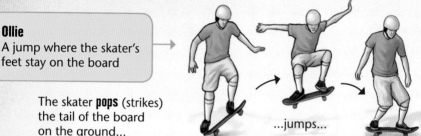

Ollie
A jump where the skater's feet stay on the board

The skater **pops** (strikes) the tail of the board on the ground...

"POP!"

...jumps...

...then lands.

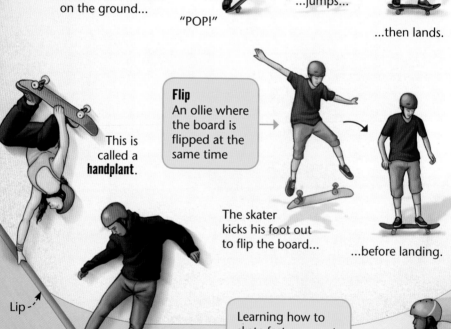

This is called a **handplant**.

Flip
An ollie where the board is flipped at the same time

The skater kicks his foot out to flip the board...

...before landing.

Lip

Lip
Part of the skateboard or skater balances on the lip (edge) or a ramp or obstacle

Learning how to skate fast on a vert ramp or flat ground is an essential skill too. Most tricks need speed to work well.

Manual
Balancing with the front or back wheels off the ground

This trick is called a **hang ten**.

Grinds and slides
The wheels, trucks or wooden deck of a skateboard slide along an obstacle.

In a **grind**, the skater uses the wheels or trucks.

Nose grab

Grab
The skater grabs the board with one or two hands.

A **slide** uses the wooden deck.

Indy grab
(between feet)

This is an **airwalk**, where the skater grabs the board's nose, then sticks both legs out to the side.

In an **air spin**, the skater and board rotate.

Air
The board and rider jump and perform a trick in the air before landing, usually on a vert ramp.

Urban extremes

Here are some other extreme sports that use skateparks, vert ramps and street obstacles to ride, race or perform tricks.

Freestyle scootering

- A cross between skateboarding and BMX freestyle (see pages 10-13), scooters are used to perform tricks in skateparks, vert ramps and on flat street surfaces.

Aggressive inline skating

- Skateboarding-style street tricks done wearing inline skates.

Inline skates are boots with 4 wheels in a line along the sole.

Longboarding

- A longboard skateboard is used to race downhill, slalom (weave in and out of obstacles), or perform tricks.
- Longboards are longer and more stable than standard skateboards – 84-150cm (33-59in), compared to 71-81cm (28-31in) for skateboards.

Hands and feet help to steer around sharp bends.

Parkour

- Finding new and inventive ways of getting from one obstacle to the next (often in a town or city), using just the body.
- Participants are known as traceurs or traceuses.

Cat leap

The traceuse runs up to a wall and jumps up, grabbing the top of the wall before pulling herself on top of it.

Precision jump

Balancing on the edge of a roof, the traceuse spots her landing point. She jumps, using her arms to balance, before landing.

Forward flip

Sometimes, a traceuse will do an acrobatic move, such as a flip.

Speed vault

She uses one hand to steady herself while jumping over an obstacle.

Roll

Rolling after landing a jump absorbs the impact and allows the traceuse to travel fluidly to the next move.

Mountain high

Pulling yourself up a rock wall far from the ground, climbing requires a steady nerve, strong muscles, quick thinking and control.

Free climbing

Traditional rock climbing is known as free climbing because the climber uses just his hands and feet to move up. Equipment is there to protect the climber if he falls.

1 **Harness:** Attaches the climber to the rope via a metal loop called a **carabiner**. Other equipment is clipped onto the harness, too.

2 **Chalk bag:** The climber rubs his hands with chalk to improve grip. He can also wrap around tape or bandages for extra protection.

3 **Protection devices:** These anchor the climber's rope to the rock during a climb. Find out more on pages 50-51.

4 **Climbing shoes**

5 **Rope**

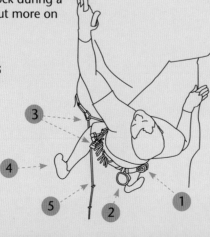
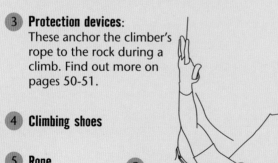

Here, free climber Elijah Weber is making his way up a difficult climbing route called Yellow Wall, at the City of Rocks National Reserve, in Idaho, USA.

The grip a climber uses and the place where he grips the rock is called a **hold**.

Free climbing

- **Records: Fastest climb:** 2 hours, 43 minutes, 33 seconds to climb 883m (2,900ft), Hans Florine (USA) and Yuji Hirayama (Japan), El Capitan, Yosemite National Park, California, USA, December 18, 2009
- **Greatest distance in 24 hours:** 8.88km (29,130ft), Will Levandowski (USA), Flagstaff Mountain near Boulder, Colorado, USA, May 4-5 2011
- **Major events:** IFSC World Cup, UIAA Championships. Climbing is also on the shortlist to be included in the Olympic Games from 2020

Essential equipment

Here's how climbers' equipment keeps them safe during a climb.

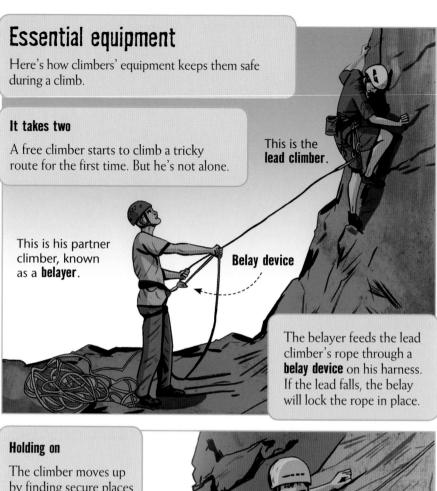

It takes two

A free climber starts to climb a tricky route for the first time. But he's not alone.

This is the **lead climber**.

This is his partner climber, known as a **belayer**.

Belay device

The belayer feeds the lead climber's rope through a **belay device** on his harness. If the lead falls, the belay will lock the rope in place.

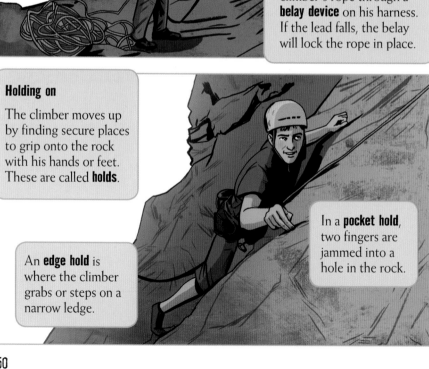

Holding on

The climber moves up by finding secure places to grip onto the rock with his hands or feet. These are called **holds**.

In a **pocket hold**, two fingers are jammed into a hole in the rock.

An **edge hold** is where the climber grabs or steps on a narrow ledge.

After around 20m (65ft), the lead climber wedges a **protection device** into a crack in the rock.

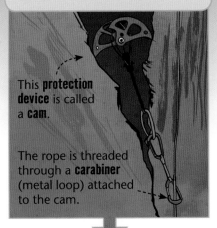

This **protection device** is called a **cam**.

The rope is threaded through a **carabiner** (metal loop) attached to the cam.

Up the rock face, the rope is pulled taught through the cam so the climber doesn't slip very far.

He swings himself up to reach a hold above his head...

...but, he slips!

On the ground, the belayer pulls down on the rope so it locks still in the belay device.

SNAP!

Hard rocks

Experienced climbers look for the most challenging climbing routes on which to test their skills.

Grading system

All climbing routes are **graded** on a scale. In the US, the scale goes from grades 1 to 5. An extra 0.1 points and the letters a-d are added to show increasing difficulty within a grade. The hardest route is currently graded 5.15c+. The first to climb a route gets to grade and name it.

Nit de Bruixes Margalef, Spain

- **Route:** 25m (82ft) arch
- **Grade:** 5.15a
- **First climbed:** Iker Pou (Spain), January 2012
- **Difficulty:** shallow, one finger holds along horizontal sections. Rock can be unstable and prone to crumbling.

The Change Flatanger Cave, Norway

- **Route:** 55m (180ft) granite arch
- **Grade:** 5.15c+
- **First climbed:** Adam Ondra (Czech Republic), October 2012. Adam Ondra and Chris Sharma (USA) have climbed some of the most difficult routes in the world today.

- 45-60° overhanging walls
- Horizontal section

Realization/Biographie
Montagne de Céüse, France

- **Route:** 35m (115ft) limestone wall
- **Grade:** 5.15a
- **First climbed:** Chris Sharma (USA), July 2001

- Smooth, vertical walls with few obvious holds or cracks for protection devices

Jumbo Love Clark's Mountain, California, USA

- **Route:** 27m (250ft) overhang
- **Grade:** 5.15b
- **First climbed:** Chris Sharma (USA), July 2008

- 45° overhanging rock wall with shallow holds and few cracks

La Dura Dura (the Hard Hard)
Oliana, Spain

- **Route:** 50m (165ft) overhanging rock
- **Grade:** 5.15c
- **First climbed:** Adam Ondra (Czech Republic), February 2013. Chris Sharma completed the second ascent of La Dura Dura the following month.

- Smooth rock face with wide gaps between holds

Soloing

Soloing is a type of extreme climbing done in different locations without any safety ropes, harnesses or protection devices.

This is free soloist Mich Kemeter, 300m (1,000ft) up a canyon wall while solo climbing in the Verdon National Park, France.

Deep water soloing

- Soloing along sea cliffs or valley rock walls above deep water.

The climber has water to break their fall.

A boulder is usually no more than 6m (20ft) tall.

Bouldering

- Soloing on low rock formations (boulders).
- A route, known as a problem, is climbed across each boulder within a specific number of moves.

Buildering

- Solo climbing to the top of tall buildings.
- As an extra challenge, climbs are often done at night.

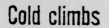

Cold climbs

Climbing up vertical, ice-covered rocks or frozen waterfalls at sub-zero temperatures, ice climbing routes are some of the hardest.

This ice climber is scaling Even Thomas Creek, a frozen waterfall in the Rocky Mountains in Canada.

Ice climbing

- **Records: Furthest distance in 24 hours:** 7746m (25,414ft), Will Gadd (Canada), Ouray Ice Festival, Colorado, USA, January 9-10 2010
- **Major events:** X Games, UIAA Ice Climbing World Tour

It's far too slippery and cold to grip the ice using hand holds. Instead, ice climbers carry an **ice tool** in each hand and use them to swing into the ice.

Ice tool ---

A **helmet, gloves** and warm, **padded clothing** are essential.

Ice screws anchor the ropes to the ice, similar to free climbing **protection devices** (see page 51 for more information).

Spiked soles, called **crampons,** are attached to shoes. The climber kicks his foot into the ice so the spikes get a firm hold.

Riders on the snow

Snowboarding is the extreme sport of speeding down snow-covered slopes on a smooth wooden board.

Racing

Snowboard races are super-fast downhill contests. The first over the finish line wins.

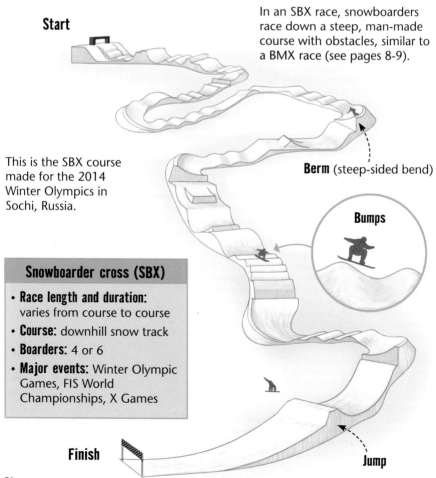

Start

In an SBX race, snowboarders race down a steep, man-made course with obstacles, similar to a BMX race (see pages 8-9).

This is the SBX course made for the 2014 Winter Olympics in Sochi, Russia.

Berm (steep-sided bend)

Bumps

Snowboarder cross (SBX)

- **Race length and duration:** varies from course to course
- **Course:** downhill snow track
- **Boarders:** 4 or 6
- **Major events:** Winter Olympic Games, FIS World Championships, X Games

Finish

Jump

Parallel giant slalom

- **Race length:** around 500m (1,600ft) with 35 gates 20-27m (65-88ft) apart
- **Vertical drop:** 120-200m (390-650ft)
- **Course:** downhill snow track
- **Boarders:** 2
- **Major events:** Winter Olympic Games, FIS World Championships, X Games

Slalom snowboarders race downhill, zig-zagging through gates on parallel courses. This is what a typical slalom course looks like:

The boarder makes fast, arching turns around the gates. This is called **carving**.

Goggles and **helmets** are worn for protection.

Snowboarders' feet are strapped into **boots** that are already **bound** (fixed) to the board.

A **gate** is a tall pole connected to a short pole by a triangular panel.

59

Freestyle

Freestyle snowboarders perform complex routines of tricks, called runs, that include jumps, flips, spins and slides. There are four different types of freestyle events.

This boarder is doing a **grab** trick, similar to a skateboarding grab.

Event	Venue	Competition	Major events
Big Mountain Freeride	Steep downhill mountain trail with obstacles	1 run Judging criteria: • difficulty of path chosen • execution of tricks • general style	• Tailgate Alaska • Red Bull Powder Escape • North Face Masters • Freeride World Tour
Slopestyle	Man-made downhill course with obstacles	2 runs Judging criteria: • variety, difficulty and execution of tricks • amplitude (height gained)	• Winter Olympic Games • Winter X Games • Ticket to Ride World Snowboarding Tour • Air & Style • Shakedown • US Open of Snowboarding

Competitors in **Big Mountain events** look for obstacles, such as ramps or rocky outcrops where they can slide, or jump and flip.

Event	Venue	Competition	Major events
Big Air	Big Air ramp with a minimum height of 35m (114ft) 	3 runs Judging criteria: • difficulty and execution of tricks • amplitude • control • landing	• World Extreme Snowboarding Championships • Winter X Games • Ticket to Ride World Snowboarding Tour • Air & Style
Half-pipe	Half-pipe (u-shaped bowl)	2 runs Judging criteria: • difficulty and execution of tricks • amplitude • flow • creativity	• Winter Olympic Games • Winter X Games • Ticket to Ride World Snowboarding Tour • Shakedown • Air & Style • US Open of Snowboarding

Watery extremes

Surfing, the sport of riding sea waves, has been around for thousands of years. Now, surfers travel the world in search of the perfect waves.

A surfer balances on a **surfboard** as he's pushed along by the force of a wave. He tries to surf to the shore before the wave breaks (crashes down) on top of him.

Surfing

- **Records: Longest wave surfed:** 66.47km (41.3 miles) over 3 hours, 55 minutes, Panama Canal, Panama, Gary Saavedra (Panama), March 19, 2011
- **Major events:** Association of Surfing Professionals (ASP) World Tour, the Rip Curl Pro, the Billabong Pro, the Quicksilver Pro, Triple Crown of Surfing

The story of surfing

Surfing began thousands of years ago in the Polynesian Islands of the Pacific Ocean. Fisherman used waves as a speedy way to reach the shore.

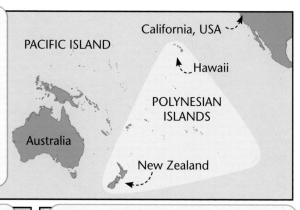

PACIFIC ISLAND

California, USA

Hawaii

POLYNESIAN ISLANDS

Australia

New Zealand

In Hawaii, the best surfers challenged each other to surfing contests.

They surfed on long, heavy boards carved from trees.

At the start of the 20th century, Hawaiian surfers came to California, USA, and Australia to show off their amazing skills.

At this time, designers made lighter boards that were easier to control.

Duke Kahanamoku was one of the best Hawaiian surfers.

By the 1950s and 60s, surfing had become extremely popular. Some people made it a way of life, driving up and down coasts looking for the best waves.

Let's go surfing now!

If someone wants to go surfing, the first thing they do is check that conditions are right.

There are surfing forecast sites that track wave conditions around the world.

The best waves for surfing curl up to make a wall of water. This is known as a **tube** or **barrel wave**.

Surf's up means that waves are good for surfing.

Which board?

Next, a surfer has to choose which board to use, and get ready to take it into the sea.

Longboards
2.7-3.7m (9-12ft) long. Slower, but easier to surf in calmer seas with smaller waves.

Shortboards
1.5-2.1m (5-7ft) long. Quick and better for surfing big, powerful waves.

A **leash** stops the board from floating away from the surfer if he falls off.

Fins keep the board straight in the water.

Adding **wax** to the surface will help feet to grip.

Out at sea

1. The surfer paddles away from the shore. He sits on the board, waiting for a good surfing wave.

This is known as **catching the wave.**

2. As a wave approaches, he paddles fast to catch up with it.

3. He brings his legs up under his body, pops his feet up on the board, and stands up.

4. Keeping his knees bent helps him to balance.

Tricks

Before the wave breaks, he tries some impressive moves and tricks.

Tubing: riding through the 'tube' of the wave

Airs: launching the board off the top of a wave

Carving: swerving in and out of the face of the wave

Hang ten: walking to the front of the board and wrapping all ten toes around the end

The biggest waves

Some surfers specialize in only the biggest and most dangerous waves, the ones that are over 6m (20ft) tall.

Around the world

Big surfing waves only happen in certain places around the world, usually after stormy weather. Some places have become famous for their waves.

Name/location	Wave size	Famous for
1 Mavericks and Ghost Trees, California, USA	15-21m (50-70ft)	Maverick's Surf Contest, where the best big wave surfers from around the world compete
2 Waimei Bay and Pipeline, Oahu, Hawaii, USA	6-9m (20-30ft)	The Triple Crown of Surfing contest. Big waves breaking into dangerous shallow water
3 Teahupoo, Tahiti, French Polynesia	up to 7m (21ft)	Tall waves breaking in massive tubes. The ASP World Tour Event challenges surfers to ride them
4 Praia do Norte, Nazaré, Portugal	over 27m (90ft)	The biggest wave ever surfed: 23.77m (78ft), Garrett McNamara (USA), November 1, 2011
5 Dungeons, nr. Cape Town, South Africa	up to 14m (47ft)	The Red Bull Big Wave Africa competition
6 Cyclops, Western Australia	over 6m (20ft)	Australia's biggest and most dangerous surfing waves

7 Peahi (Jaws)

- **Where:** Maui, Hawaii, USA
- **Waves:** over 18m (60ft)
- **Famous for:** the Red Bull Jaws contest, in which 21 of the best big wave surfers compete against each other

Towing in

Big waves only happen in very rough seas. Some surfers paddle in, but most are towed into waves by holding onto a strong cable attached to a jet ski or helicopter.

Riding **dropknee** is crouching with one foot up on the board.

Out at sea

Here are some more extreme water sports influenced by surfing:

Bodyboarding

- **Aim:** to ride a wave and/or perform tricks while lying prone (on the stomach) or kneeling on a bodyboard
- **Equipment:** short, rectangular foam board
- **Major events:** International Bodyboarding Association (IBA) Men's, Women's and Dropknee Tour, Pipeline Pro

Kitesurfing

- **Aim:** to steer a board across the surface of the water using wind power
- **Equipment:** board with foot straps, a power kite, body harness

- **Records: Fastest:** 103km/h (64mph), Rob Douglas (USA), October 28, 2010
- **Major events:** Kiteboarding World Cup, International Kiteboarding Association Tour Championships

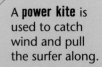

A **power kite** is used to catch wind and pull the surfer along.

The kitesurfer changes the position of his body and board to steer through the water. He can perform tricks, such as flips, too.

Foot straps keep the kitesurfer secured to the board.

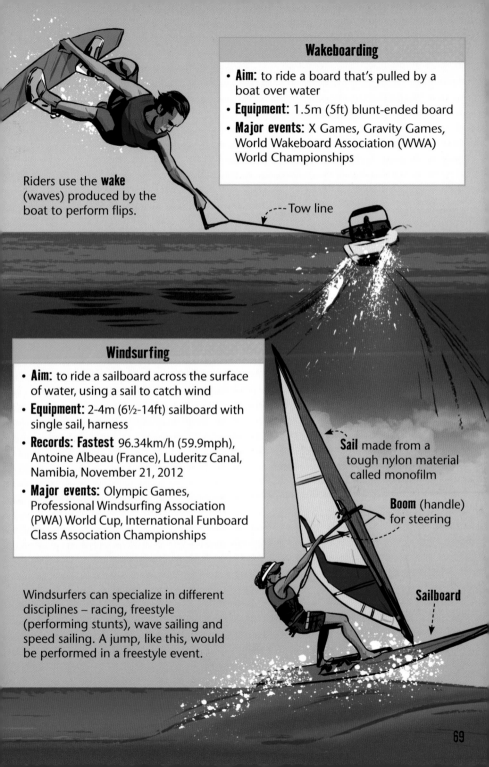

Wakeboarding

- **Aim:** to ride a board that's pulled by a boat over water
- **Equipment:** 1.5m (5ft) blunt-ended board
- **Major events:** X Games, Gravity Games, World Wakeboard Association (WWA) World Championships

Riders use the **wake** (waves) produced by the boat to perform flips.

----Tow line

Windsurfing

- **Aim:** to ride a sailboard across the surface of water, using a sail to catch wind
- **Equipment:** 2-4m (6½-14ft) sailboard with single sail, harness
- **Records: Fastest** 96.34km/h (59.9mph), Antoine Albeau (France), Luderitz Canal, Namibia, November 21, 2012
- **Major events:** Olympic Games, Professional Windsurfing Association (PWA) World Cup, International Funboard Class Association Championships

Sail made from a tough nylon material called monofilm

Boom (handle) for steering

Windsurfers can specialize in different disciplines – racing, freestyle (performing stunts), wave sailing and speed sailing. A jump, like this, would be performed in a freestyle event.

Sailboard

Whitewater

Whitewater kayakers paddle down challenging river courses, either racing against the clock, or navigating around dangerous obstacles.

Kayaks are small, narrow boats with a cockpit for one pilot.

Helmet

Pilot

A **spray skirt** or **deck** is waterproof material that fits around the pilot and over the cockpit. It keeps the pilot in, and water out.

Personal flotation device (PFD)

Cockpit

Bags filled with air inside the boat stop it from sinking.

Tough carbon **paddles** to push the kayak through the water

This slalom kayaker is training on a course on the Isère river in France.

River grades

Whitewater is rapids water that froths and bubbles. In kayaking, a river is given a **grade** from I to VI according to how difficult or dangerous it is. Grade VI rivers are so severe they're classed as 'life-threatening'.

Grade I

Grade VI

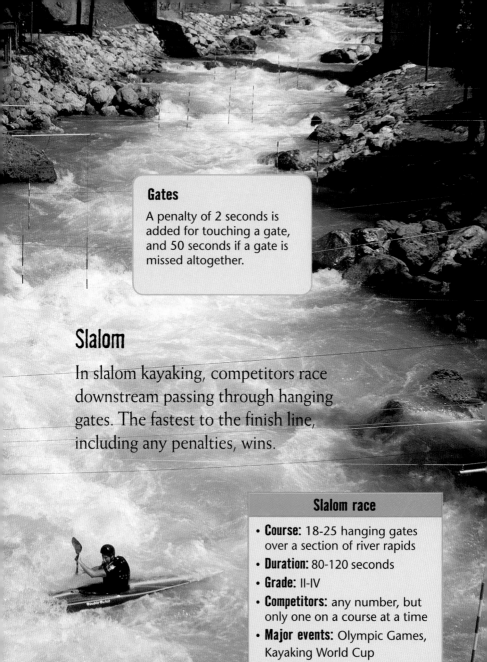

Gates

A penalty of 2 seconds is added for touching a gate, and 50 seconds if a gate is missed altogether.

Slalom

In slalom kayaking, competitors race downstream passing through hanging gates. The fastest to the finish line, including any penalties, wins.

Slalom race

- **Course:** 18-25 hanging gates over a section of river rapids
- **Duration:** 80-120 seconds
- **Grade:** II-IV
- **Competitors:** any number, but only one on a course at a time
- **Major events:** Olympic Games, Kayaking World Cup

Up the creek

Creeking is a type of whitewater kayaking where pilots navigate down steep river rapids, graded IV to VI.

At the top of the river is a steep, smooth channel of rock with shallow water running over it. This is a slide.

The pilot launches the kayak down the slide. It's pushed along the rock by the fast-running water.

He steers the kayak straight by using different paddle strokes on one side of the boat, then the other.

Up ahead, a tree has fallen across the river.

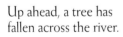

The pilot paddles to the edge of the river, climbs out, and carries his boat past the tree.

Once he's back in the water, there's an especially difficult obstacle for the pilot to tackle – a waterfall. He paddles over the edge.

As he's falling, he pulls his legs up to lift the front of the kayak...

...so that when it lands, the front of the kayak stays up above the water. This is called boofing.

Now in deeper water, the kayak is flipped over by a strong surge of water.

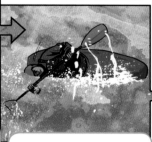

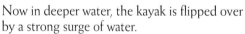

He reaches his paddle up onto the bottom of the kayak....

...twists his body up into a 'c' shape...

...then uses his body and arms to pull the kayak upright.

Ultra extreme

Some sports are extreme because they're an ultimate test of strength and endurance.

An ultramarathon is an exhausting race where runners compete to finish a very long course — anywhere between 50km (31 miles) and 160km (100 miles).

This runner is competing in the Dubai stage of the Desert Cup, an ultramarathon that passes through four deserts across the world.

Extreme sports on the internet

For links to websites where you can find out more about the different extreme sports, the competitions where you can see them first hand, and even how you can get involved, go to the Usborne Quicklinks website at **www.usborne.com/quicklinks** and enter the keywords: **extreme sports**.

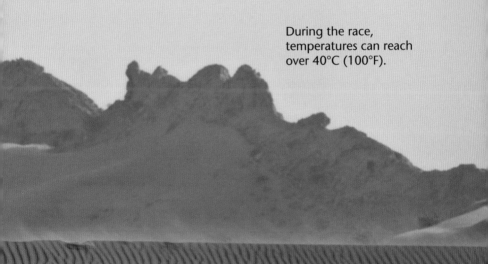

During the race, temperatures can reach over 40°C (100°F).

Glossary

This glossary explains some of the words used in this book.
If a word is written in *italic* type, it has an entry of its own.

air A *trick* in which a person and his or her equipment jump into the air.

altimeter A device that tells a *skydiver* how far from the ground he or she is.

BASE jump A low *skydive* done from different Earth-based objects.

belay To keep a *free climber's* rope secure during a climb, usually with the help of a partner climber.

berm A steep-sided bend.

bungee jump A jump from a high platform while attached to an elastic bungee cord.

BMX The sport of riding BMX (bicycle motocross) bikes.

canopy A parachute.

carve To do a sharp, quick turn across snow or water.

deployment The release of a *skydiving* or *BASE jumping canopy*.

discipline A sub-category of a sport that has its own set of rules and *events*.

DZ (dropzone) The place where a skydiver aims to land at the end of a jump.

event A competition.

free climbing Climbing up rock or ice using safety equipment.

freefall During a *skydive* jump, the period before the *canopy* is *deployed*.

freestyle The *discipline* of a sport that involves *tricks*.

gate Two parallel poles that a *kayaker* or *snowboarder* has to pass through or around in a *slalom* race.

grab A *trick* that involves grabbing a piece of equipment with one or both hands.

grind A *trick* in which the wheels or *truck* on a skateboard, or the bottom of a snowboard, slide against an obstacle.

hang gliding Flying a non-motorized v-shaped *wing* through the air, using wind power to stay up.

hold The way that a climber grips the surface being climbed. It's also the name for the parts of the surface that can be gripped onto.

ice climbing The *free climbing* of an ice-covered surface.

jump An obstacle that makes a person and their equipment jump into the air.

kayaking Paddling a small, narrow boat called a kayak across water, often through hazardous *whitewater*.

kite buggying The sport of driving a wheeled buggy that's powered by a wide *canopy*, called a kite.

lift A force that keeps people and their equipment up in the air.

lip The edge of an obstacle and any *tricks* that involve the lip.

manual Riding on two wheels of a skateboard, or one wheel of a bike.

MTB (mountain biking) The sport of riding a mountain bike.

paragliding Flying a *wing canopy* for as long as possible through the air.

park A purpose-built area with obstacles where BMX freestyle riders or skaters perform tricks.

parkour Moving up onto, across and down from obstacles using just your body.

pilot chute A small *canopy* that helps to inflate the *canopy* during a *skydive* or *BASE jump*.

protection devices Equipment to stop a *free climber* from falling too far during a climb.

run A routine made up of a set number of *tricks* in *freestyle events*.

skateboarding The sport of riding a wheeled board and performing *tricks* on it.

skydiving The sport of jumping from an aircraft, then using a *canopy* to float to the ground.

slalom A race that involves passing through a number of *gates*.

slide A *trick* in which the wooden part of a skateboard slides against an obstacle.

snowboarding The sport of riding a snowboard – either in a race or in *freestyle events*.

solo climbing Climbing done without any safety equipment.

street A *discipline* where *tricks* are performed on obstacles you might find in a street, such as handrails.

surfing The sport of riding a surfboard across the surface of a wave.

suspension Part of a bike that deals with shocks and jolts to give a smooth ride.

tread The patterns of grooves in a bike wheel to improve grip.

trials A *mountain bike discipline* which involves riders navigating a course of obstacles without stepping on the ground.

trick A stunt, such as a flip, done in *freestyle events*.

truck The part of a skateboard that attaches the wheels to the board.

vert ramp A u-shaped ramp used in some *BMX*, *skateboarding* and *snowboarding disciplines*.

whitewater Hazardous, fast-flowing river water with lots of obstacles.

wing A type of *canopy* for *hang gliding* and *paragliding* designed to stay up in the air for as long as possible.

wingsuit flying A *skydive* or *BASE jump* done wearing a modified jumpsuit.

XC (cross country) A long race across rough terrain.

Index

Acknowledgements

Every effort has been made to trace and acknowledge ownership of copyright. If any rights have been omitted, the publishers offer to rectify this in any future editions following notification. The publishers are grateful to the following individuals and organizations for permission to reproduce material on the following pages:

cover © Duomo/Corbis; **p1** © Digital Vision/Thinkstock; **p2-3** © Erik Aeder/ Getty Images; **p4-5** © James Balog/Getty Images; **p6** © Niels Poulsen sprt/ Alamy; **p7** © Christoph Jorda /Corbis; **p10-11** © GoodSportHD.com/Alamy; **p14-15** © Dan Barham/Getty Images; **p18** © Fabienne Krummenacher, Switzerland; **p20-21** © Norman Kent; **p24** © Red Bull Stratos; **p26-27** © Jeff Gilbert/Alamy; **p31** © O Furrer/F1 ONLINE/SuperStock; **p32** © Tips Images/SuperStock; **p34** © Gary Crabbe/Enlightened Images/Alamy; **p35** © Olivier Parent/Alamy; **p38-39** © Trevor Clark/Getty Images; **p40** © Jared Wickerham/Stringer/Getty Images; **p41** © Bo Bridges/Corbis; **p48-49** © Mark Weber/age fotostock/SuperStock; **p52-53** © Alberto Lessmann/Red Bull Content Pool; **p54** © Alexandre Buisse http://www.alexandrebuisse.org; **p56-57** © Ryan Creary/All Canada Photos/Corbis; **p59** © Aflo Co. Ltd / Alamy; **p60-61** © Julian Love/JAI/Corbis; **p62** © shannonstent/Getty Images; **p67** © Ron Dahlquist/Getty Images; **p71** © Aurora Photos/Alamy; **p74-75** © Jürgen Skarwan/Red Bull Content Pool.

Additional illustrations by Zoe Wray and Alice Reese
Series editor: Jane Chisholm   Series designer: Zoe Wray
Digital design by John Russell   Picture research by Ruth King